WITHDRAWN

Johnston Public Library
6700 Merle Hay Road
Johnston, Iowa 50131

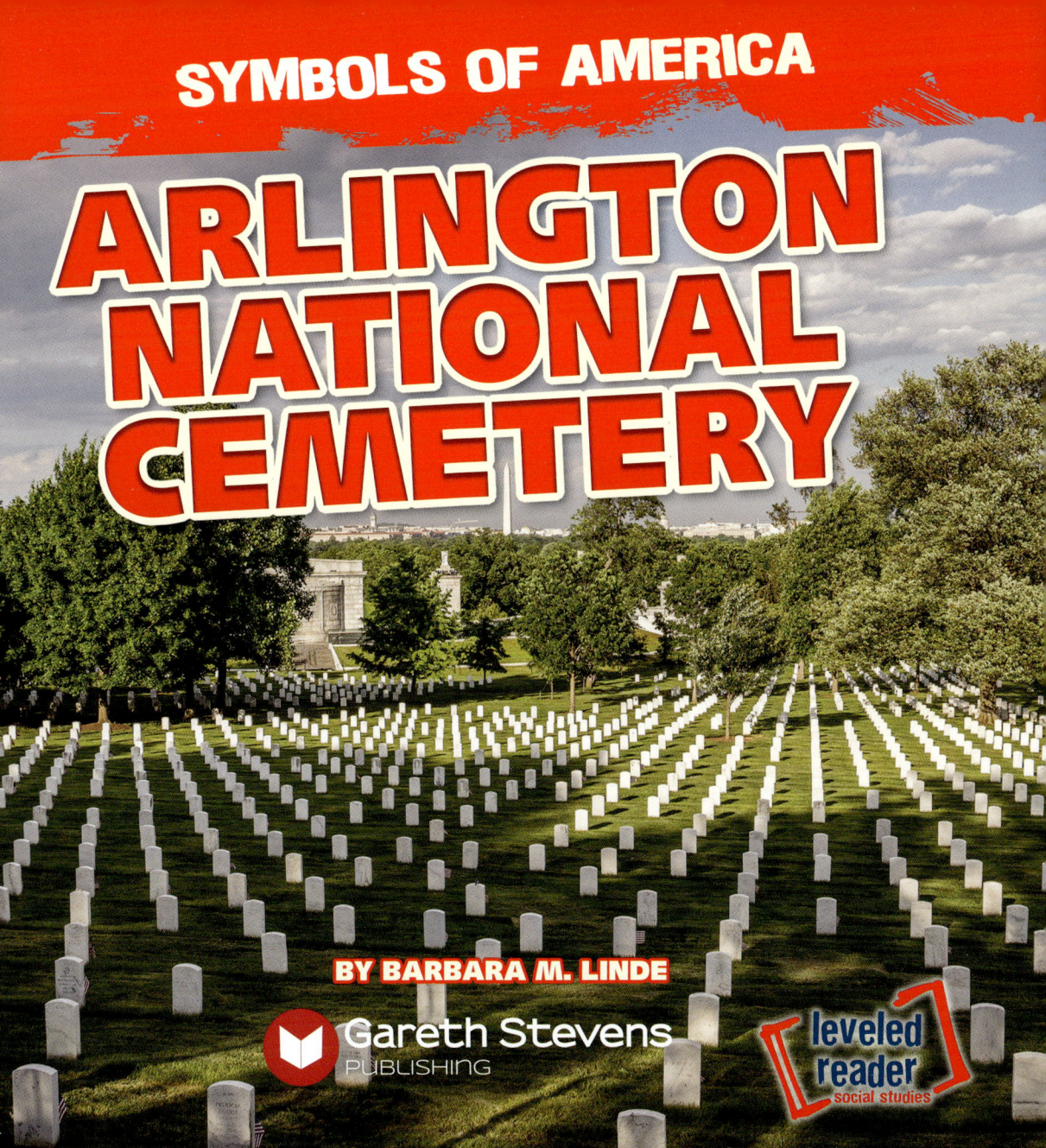

Please visit our website, www.garethstevens.com. For a free color catalog of all our high-quality books, call toll free 1-800-542-2595 or fax 1-877-542-2596.

Library of Congress Cataloging-in-Publication Data

Names: Linde, Barbara M., author.
Title: Arlington National Cemetery / Barbara M. Linde.
Description: New York : Gareth Stevens Publishing, [2019] | Series: Symbols of America | Includes index.
Identifiers: LCCN 2018014467| ISBN 9781538228975 (library bound) | ISBN 9781538232248 (pbk.) | ISBN 9781538232255 (6 pack)
Subjects: LCSH: Arlington National Cemetery (Arlington, Va.)–Juvenile literature. | Arlington (Va.)–Buildings, structures, etc.–Juvenile literature.
Classification: LCC F234.A7 L56 2019 | DDC 975.5/295–dc23
LC record available at https://lccn.loc.gov/2018014467

Published in 2019 by
Gareth Stevens Publishing
111 East 14th Street, Suite 349
New York, NY 10003

Copyright © 2019 Gareth Stevens Publishing

Designer: Sarah Liddell
Editor: Joshua Turner

Photo credits: Cover, p. 1 Guillermo Olaizola/Shutterstock.com; p. 5 Hoberman Collection/Contributor/Universal Images Group/Getty Images; p. 7 Historical/Contributor/Corbis Historical/Getty Images; p. 9 Ser Amantio di Nicolao/Wikimedia Commons; p. 11 David Kay/Shutterstock.com; p. 13 Kamira/Shutterstock.com; p. 15 Charlie Hutton/Shutterstock.com; p. 17 emkaplin/Shutterstock.com; p. 19 Alex Wong/Staff/Getty Images News/Getty Images; p. 21 Anton_Ivanov/Shutterstock.com.

All rights reserved. No part of this book may be reproduced in any form without permission in writing from the publisher, except by a reviewer.

Printed in the United States of America

CPSIA compliance information: Batch #CW19GS: For further information contact Gareth Stevens, New York, New York at 1-800-542-2595.

CONTENTS

A National Cemetery 4

The Need for Arlington 6

The Peaceful Grounds 8

Military from Other Wars 10

The Unknown Soldier 12

President John F. Kennedy 14

Astronauts 16

Special Ceremonies 18

Visit Arlington 20

Glossary 22

For More Information 23

Index 24

Boldface words appear in the glossary.

A National Cemetery

A national **cemetery** is a place where American heroes are buried. Many were **veterans**. Government leaders, astronauts, and others also are buried there. With 400,000 graves, Arlington National Cemetery is the second largest national cemetery in the United States.

The Need for Arlington

During the **Civil War**, the government turned a large piece of land in Arlington, Virginia, into a cemetery. About 16,000 Union and Confederate soldiers were buried there during and after the war. Graves for about 3,800 freed slaves were put nearby.

The Peaceful Grounds

The cemetery is built on gentle green hills. Tall trees, some of them more than 100 years old, shade the grave markers and the visitors. Gardens are full of beautiful flowers. Monuments and **memorials** honor special people and groups.

Military from Other Wars

The **American Revolution** took place before the Civil War. After the cemetery was opened, the bodies of some soldiers from the American Revolution were reburied there. **Military** members from other wars are at rest here, too. Today, there are about 7,000 **funerals** each year.

The Unknown Soldier

We do not know the names of all of the soldiers who died in wars. The **Tomb** of the Unknown Soldier honors them. Soldiers called the Old Guard stay at the tomb all day, every day. Three soldiers at a time march back and forth.

President John F. Kennedy

John F. Kennedy was shot and killed in Dallas, Texas, on November 22, 1963, while he was still the president. Leaders from all over the world came to his funeral. A fire called the eternal flame burns near his gravesite. It never goes out.

Astronauts

Astronauts bravely travel to space, and a few times, there have been terrible accidents. The space shuttles *Challenger* and *Columbia* blew up in space. One rocket exploded before it could take off. Memorials help us remember these daring men and women.

Special Ceremonies

On Memorial Day and Veterans Day, the army lays a wreath at the Tomb of the Unknown Soldier. A military band plays, and people talk about the heroes at rest in Arlington. The president and other government leaders often take part in these services.

Visit Arlington

The cemetery is open every day. Check in first at the Welcome Center. There, you can learn more about the history of the cemetery. You can even have a parent or teacher download an app to help you find your way around!

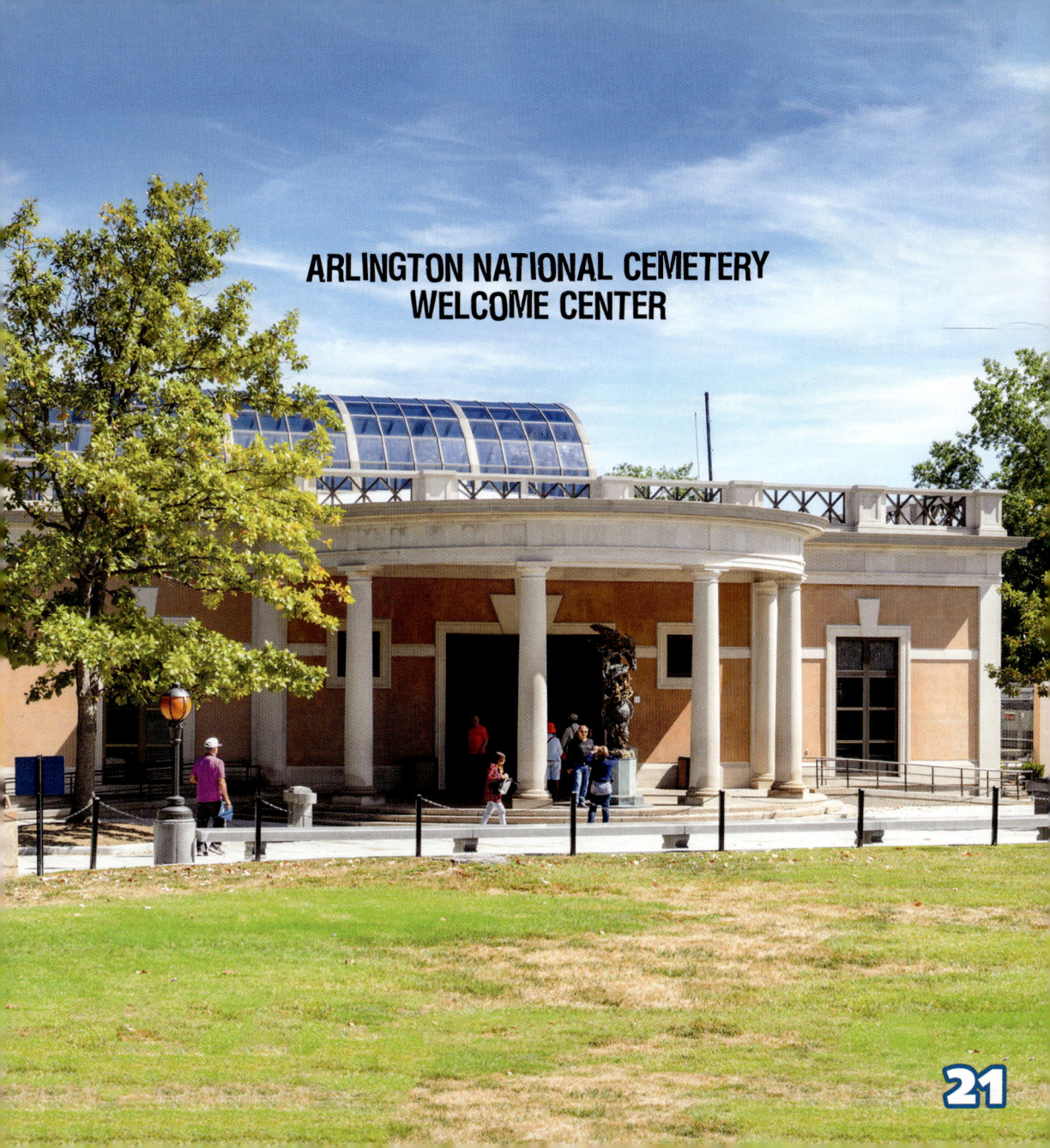

GLOSSARY

American Revolution: the war in which the colonies won their freedom from England

cemetery: a place where the dead are buried

Civil War: a war fought from 1861 to 1865 in the United States between the Union (the Northern states) and the Confederacy (the Southern states)

funeral: an event honoring a person who has died

memorial: a place, display, or event that serves as a way to remember someone

military: having to do with the army, navy, marines, air force, or coast guard

tomb: a large underground area for burying the dead

veteran: someone who fought in a war

FOR MORE INFORMATION

BOOKS

Khalid, Jinnow. *Arlington National Cemetery and the Tomb of the Unknown Soldier.* New York: PowerKids Press, 2017.

Temple, Bob. *Arlington National Cemetery.* North Mankato, MN; Child's World Inc., 2014.

WEBSITES

Arlington National Cemetery
www.arlingtoncemetery.mil/#/
Learn more about our nation's cemetery on the official website.

Arlington National Cemetery
www.nps.gov/nr/travel/national_cemeteries/virginia/arlington_national_cemetery.html
Take a virtual trip to the cemetery or plan your visit with the National Park Service's website.

Publisher's note to educators and parents: Our editors have carefully reviewed these websites to ensure that they are suitable for students. Many websites change frequently, however, and we cannot guarantee that a site's future contents will continue to meet our high standards of quality and educational value. Be advised that students should be closely supervised whenever they access the internet.

INDEX

American Revolution 10

astronauts 4, 16

Challenger 16

Civil War 6, 10

Columbia 16

eternal flame 14

funerals 10, 14

graves 4, 6, 8, 14

heroes 4, 18

Kennedy, John F. 14

Memorial Day 18

memorials 8, 16

military 10, 18

monument 8

Old Guard 12

slaves 6

soldiers 6, 10, 12, 18

tomb 12, 18

veterans 4

Veterans Day 18